All About Families

Who's in your family?

Me with Mom, Grandpa and Bella

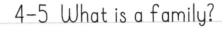

Contents

The Khan family

The Coopers

Ahmed's family

Our new baby

My cat Dusty

My family

My auntie's cat

My cousin's treehouse

Usborne

All About Families

Felicity Brooks

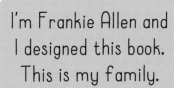

I'm Mar Ferrero and I did the illustrations. Here's my family.

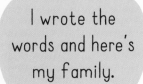
I wrote the words and here's my family.

I'm Frankie Allen and I designed this book. This is my family.

What is a family?

Maybe you know a family that looks a little like the one in this picture, but families may also look like these...

Hello!

or these ...

Hi!

or these ...

Hello!

or these . . .

or these . . .

or these . . .

Hello!

or these.

All shapes and sizes

Families come in all shapes and sizes and **every single one** is different, all over the world.

A family may be very BIG...

...or a family can be just two people (and their pets).

The people in a family may look a lot like each other...

...or they may all look a little different.

The people in a family can be short ...

... or they may all be tall.

Or they could be a mixture.

The people in families may all like to wear different clothes.

Hej Carla!

Hello Dad!

They may all enjoy doing different things ...

... and some speak different languages.

Who's in your family?

These children are all in the same class at school. They've drawn some pictures and are talking about who's in their families.

I'm Valentine and I live with two cats, my mom and dad and my brother, Alfie.

I'm Freddie and I have two dads. They adopted me when I was a baby.

That means the right family was found for him when he needed one.

I'm Megan and I live mainly with my mom and sister, Bethan. We see our dad some weekends.

I'm Billy and I live with my sister and dad. My mom died when I was little.

If you're an orphan like me, it means both your parents have died.

Hi! I'm Alesha. I live with my mom and grandpa. Our dog's name is Bella.

I'm Lily and I live with my moms, Sally and Becky.

Actually my full name is Isabella von Issington the Third.

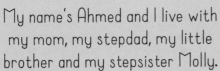
My name's Ahmed and I live with my mom, my stepdad, my little brother and my stepsister Molly.

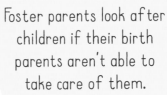
I'm Vijay, and Sanjay is my twin brother. We live with our foster parents, Alison and Ali.

Foster parents look after children if their birth parents aren't able to take care of them.

Who's in your family?
Can you draw a picture of them?

Talking about families

Because there are so many different kinds of families, people use special words to talk about them. This is what some of these words mean.

A **single parent family** is one where just a mom or a dad takes care of the children most or all of the time.

Hope I don't lose the rings!

Couples who are **married** have made important promises to each other at a **wedding** ceremony.

Grandmother

Grandfather

In some families, children are raised by their grandparents, an aunt or uncle or a grown-up brother or sister. This is called a **kinship care family**.

Brother

Sister

Not all parents are married. Some are **partners**. They may get married after they have children, or they may not.

I was adopted too.

If you're **adopted**, a new family was found for you because your **birth parents** couldn't take care of you.

Foster mom

A **foster family** looks after children if their **birth family** is not able to. This can be for a short time or a long time.

Auntie May

Oh, hurry up Uncle Rick!

Cousin Angus

Grandma Petra

And I am your great-uncle, Richard Rollington-Splange.

Great-aunt Floss

You can find out more about names for relatives on page 15.

Your **extended family** may include aunts, uncles, cousins, grandparents, great-grandparents and so on. These people are all your **relatives**.

How families can change

Families don't always stay the same. The family that you start with may change as you grow up. It could get bigger, or change in other ways.

If your family has a new baby, you have a **little brother** or **little sister**. This means you become a **big brother** or a **big sister**.

Two bedrooms! Yay!

If parents are **separated**, they aren't living together anymore, but they are still part of the family.

Mom's house

Dad's house

If parents don't want to be married or live together anymore, they may get **divorced**. They help their children through the changes this brings.

These are your grown-up stepbrothers and stepsisters.

If parents aren't together anymore and one has a new **partner**, the children may have a **step parent** or **step siblings**.

When someone **dies**, a family loses one of its members. This makes everyone in the family feel very sad because a person they love isn't there any more.

If a parent has a baby with a new partner, the other children have a **half-brother** or **half-sister** and become half-brothers or half-sisters.

If a parent has a new partner who already has children, the two families may join together to make a **blended** or **patchwork** family.

13

A family tree

A good way to show how the people in a family fit together is to draw a family tree. Here's one for a boy named Sam.

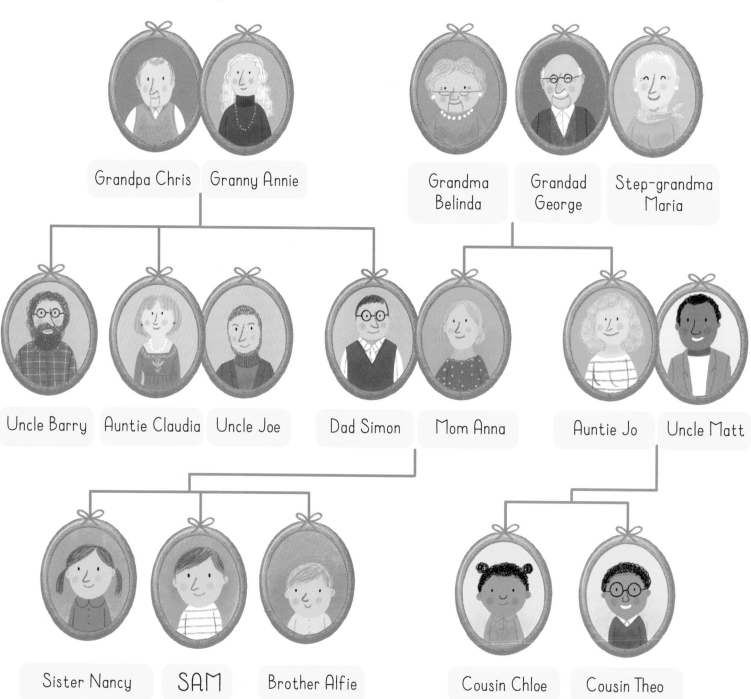

Can you draw a family tree?

The people in your family tree are all your relatives and you'll hear lots of different names for them. It's complicated, but if you do want to know these names, this shows how Sam and some of his family are related.

Grandparents

 Grandpa Chris   Granny Annie   Grandma Belinda   Grandad George   Step-grandma Maria

Sam's grandfather,
Granny's husband,
Dad's father,
Mom's father-in-law

Sam's grandmother,
Grandpa's wife,
Dad's mother,
Mom's mother-in-law

Sam's grandmother,
Grandad's ex-wife,
Mom's mother,
Dad's mother-in-law

Sam's grandfather,
Grandma's ex-husband,
Step-grandma's husband,
Mom's father,
Dad's father-in-law

Sam's step-grandmother,
Grandad's wife,
Mom's stepmother,
Dad's stepmother-in-law

Parents, aunts and uncles

 Dad Simon   Mom Anna   Auntie Jo   Uncle Matt

Sam's father,
Mom's husband,
Chris and Annie's son,
Barry and Claudia's brother,
Chloe and Theo's uncle,
Auntie Jo's brother-in-law,
George and Belinda's son-in-law,
Maria's stepson-in-law

Sam's mother,
Dad's wife,
George and Belinda's daughter,
Auntie Jo's sister,
Chloe and Theo's aunt,
Uncle Matt's sister-in-law,
Chris and Annie's daughter-in-law,
Maria's stepdaughter

Sam's aunt,
Mom's sister,
Uncle Matt's wife,
Chloe and Theo's mother,
George and Belinda's daughter,
Dad's sister-in-law,
Maria's stepdaughter

Sam's uncle,
Auntie Jo's husband,
Chloe and Theo's father,
George and Belinda's son-in-law,
Mom's brother-in-law,
Maria's stepson-in-law

Children and grandchildren

 Sister Nancy    SAM   Cousin Chloe   Cousin Theo

Sam's sister,
her parents' daughter,
her grandparents' grandaughter,
her aunt and uncle's niece,
her cousins' cousin,
her step-grandma's
step-grandaughter

Sam is Nancy and Alfie's brother,
his parents' son,
his grandparents' grandson,
his aunt and uncle's nephew,
his cousins' cousin,
his step-grandma's
step-grandson

Sam's cousin,
Auntie Jo and Uncle Matt's daughter,
Theo's sister,
Mom and Dad's niece,
her grandparents' grandaughter,
her step-grandma's
step-grandaughter

Sam's cousin,
Auntie Jo and Uncle Matt's son,
Chloe's brother,
Mom and Dad's nephew,
his grandparents' grandson,
his step-grandma's
step-grandson

Where do families live?

All families need somewhere to live, but family homes don't all look the same.

A family can live in a house . . .

a yurt . . .

or even a palace.

Many live in an apartment.

A few live in a treehouse . . .

or even a windmill.

A family can live on a farm . . .

in a camper . . .

or on a houseboat.

A family home can be in . . .

or on a tiny island in the middle of a lake.

a little village, or a town . . .

in a big, busy city . . .

Some children have two homes because their parents live in different places, or even in different countries.

Some families have nowhere to live and may be helped by friends or other people until things get more settled.

Your great-great-great-grandmother built this cottage.

Do we have everything?

Some families get to stay in the same place for a long, long time.

Some have to move house, town or even country quite often.

What is a family for?

The people in families help and take care of each other in all kinds of ways.

"Get down, Molly!"

"My dog is always happy to see me. She makes me feel happy."

"My stepson draws amazing pictures for me."

"Wow!"

"My stepmom reads me stories and helps me with my reading."

"My dads keep me safe, and sometimes they take me to the zoo."

"Have I had my tea yet, dear?"

"My mom takes care of my nana as well as me because Nana often forgets things."

Thank you, Sophie.

"My big sister helps me put my shoes on."

"I try to cheer my mom up if she's feeling tired."

You were fantastic in your school concert today!

"My dad cooks our food, washes our clothes and takes me to school."

"My moms give me a hug when they feel proud of me."

All better now, Bella!

"My mom goes to work every day to earn money to pay for everything."

"If I feel sick, my gran gives me a hug and some medicine."

Can you think of some ways the people in your family help each other?

Family talk

Parents may come from different parts of the world and speak different languages. Or they may both have grown up in the same place and speak the same language.

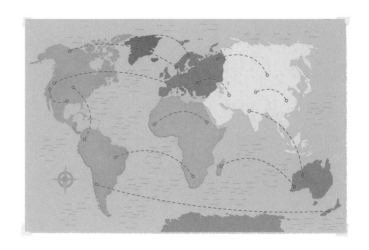

¡Hola!

¡Hola!

Carlos and Juanita both come from a village in Mexico and speak Spanish.

Hi there!

Ciao!

Mark from the USA speaks English. Simona from Italy speaks Italian.

That's cool, Grandpa!

This medal was given to me for being the best dancer in my village.

Parents and grandparents are often very proud of where they come from and like to tell their family all about it.

If your parents speak different languages, they may want you to learn both of them.

Some families use two languages at home. (The girl in the picture is saying "thank you" in American Sign Language.)

Or the children might speak one language at home and a different one at school. (These children are saying "good morning" in Welsh.)

Luckily, when you are little, you can easily learn any language and you can learn two or more at the same time.

These toddlers are all saying "Mom" in different languages. Can you guess what they are?*

*Some answers on page 32.

Family food

Everyone needs food, but different families don't eat exactly the same things, or eat in the same way.

Some families don't have a lot of choice about what they eat.

> Rice and beans

> What's for supper, Dad?

> Same as every night.

> We love paella!

> Shish kebabs are yummy!

> I like moussaka.

> Chana masala is best!

> Nasi goreng for me.

Other families have different meals every day and like to try foods from all around the world.

> Would you like some bread?

Many families are somewhere in between and sit down together to share their family meals.

But some prefer to graze and snack,

or just grab and go . . .

Celebrations

Food is often a big part of family celebrations and festivals. Sweet things are especially popular. There are ...

Cakes for birthdays

Doughnuts for Hanukkah

Cakes for weddings

Laddu for Diwali

Panettone for Christmas

Nian gao (rice cake) for Chinese New Year

Pecan pie for Thanksgiving

Butter cookies for Eid al-Fitr

Chocolate eggs for Easter

What does your family celebrate? Do you eat any special foods?

What do families do?

Many families do things together. They may . . .

go shopping,   see a movie,   or visit a museum,   a library,   a mosque, temple or church.

Some like...

going on a bus

a picnic

a game of soccer

a trip to the playground

talking to friends

a walk in the park

read a book

What does your family like to do?

walking the dog

24

going on
vacation

eating out
together

horseback
riding

rowing
a boat

feeding ducks

cycling

music

skating

meeting friends

running

25

Families and feelings

The people in a family don't always feel quite the same way about things.

And some are always arguing.

Some things can make everyone in a family feel sad.

Things that make some people feel happy can make others feel left out or jealous.

But when someone in your family says you have done something good, it can make you feel proud.

And a family can make us feel safe and loved, just by talking and doing everyday things.

Feelings can change quickly and the people in your family could be feeling all kinds of different things, sometimes all at the same time. Maybe today someone is feeling . . .

worried

upset

angry

in a good mood

excited

grumpy

proud

embarrassed

happy

But whatever your family is like today, it won't be the same as any other family in the world. Your family is special because it's different, because you are part of it, and because it's yours.

Family words

Adopted – If you're adopted, a new family was found for you because your birth parents couldn't take care of you.

Aunt/Auntie/Aunty – your mom or dad's sister, or the wife or partner of your uncle

Birth family – the family you had when you were born

Birth parents – the parents you had when you were born

Blended family – a family made up of two or more families that have joined together

Brother – a boy who has the same birth parents as you

Cousin – the son or daughter of your aunt and uncle

Daughter – If you are a girl, you are the daughter of your parents.

Divorced – A couple who is divorced used to be married but isn't any more.

Ex-husband/Ex-wife – the man/woman that a woman or man used to be married to

Extended family – your family that includes grandparents, uncles, aunts and other relatives

Family tree – a picture showing how the people in a family are connected to each other

Foster family – a family that takes care of children if the children's birth family isn't able to

Grandfather – your mom or dad's dad

Grandmother – your mom or dad's mom

Half-brother/Half-sister – a boy/girl who shares one birth parent with you

Husband – a man married to a man or woman

In-law – someone who becomes connected to a family when people marry. The wife of your brother would be your sister-in-law, for example.

Kinship care family – a family where an aunt, grown-up sister or grandparent (for example) takes care of the children

Married – A couple who is married have made important promises to each other at a wedding.

Nephew – the son of your sister or brother

Niece – the daughter of your sister or brother

Patchwork family – a family made up of two or more families that have joined together

Relatives – all the people in your extended family such as cousins, aunts and grandparents

Separated – If people in a family are separated, they don't live together any more.

Siblings – brothers and sisters

Single parent family – a family where just one mom or dad takes care of the children all or most of the time

Sister – a girl who has the same birth parents as you

Son – If you are a boy, you are the son of your parents.

Stepfamily – a family that becomes connected to you when a divorced parent marries again. The new parent is a stepmom or stepdad.

Uncle – your mom or dad's brother or the husband or partner of your aunt

Wife – a woman married to a man or woman

Index

With thanks to Anna Sharkey,
Adoption Focus (Family Society)
for expert advice

With thanks to Anna Sharkey,
Adoption Focus (Family Society)
for expert advice

Some answers to the baby languages puzzle on page 21:

Mama – Bulgarian, Greek, German, Polish, Romanian, Russian, Slovak, Spanish, Swahili, Zulu (among others)
Mom – American English   Maman – French, Persian   Mamma – Italian, Faroese, Norwegian, Swedish
Mum – British English   Mam – Welsh, Dutch, Geordie (among others)